I0104796

Copyright 2022 by BAC Learning Legacy, LLC
Text by Morgan Trace
Illustrated by Morgan Trace
Cover and Internal Design 2022 by BAC LL, LLC

All rights reserved.

Published by BAC Learning Legacy, LLC, an imprint of BAC LL, LLC.
Stone Mountain, GA 30088

The Best Pet for Me

written by Morgan Trace

I'm a mighty lion. I roar to give a fright. If you hear a mighty voice, don't venture out at night.

lion

If I'm less than fifty feet, for you there's no retreat. I devour prey with much delight, with penetrating teeth.

I'm a hungry grizzly. Looking for snacks to eat. If you see me on the trail, try not to make a peep.

When it's time to hibernate, I find a place to sleep. Walk quietly while in these woods, or the consequence is me.

grizzly bear

I'm a tiny spider. But powerful am I. Don't worry about a little bite. You're much too big to cry.

If I'm creeping down your sleeve, I'm only out to spy. Adventure's what I'm up to, when I send you my invite.

spider

I'm a tweeting birdie. I tweet with much delight. If I feel you inching close, I take to sudden flight.

Up above the treetop, I spot what I might like. That little bitty squirmy worm, I'd like to take a bite.

bird

I'm a faithful doggy, and true to you am I.
When I'm barking loud and strong, a suspect is in sight.

While I'm raging in his face, you call for 911. He's frozen stiff and begging, "Please!". I'll hold him 'til they come.

dog

I'm a little antsy. I love to search for sweets. At the park you picnic free and me you want to leave.

ant

I pick out all my favorite things, there's more than eyes can see. You throw me out before I'm done, without my favorite treats.

I'm a squiggly piglet. I oink and eat and poo. Just don't pick me as a pet. I may end up as food.

pig

You may not know, how smart I am. Your oinking is just rude. We all can't be the perfect pet. For me, I'm not for you.

I'm a clever fox-ster. I'd know if news, were new, If you catch me rambling, it's just to find a clue.

fox

Your garbage can is first to take a tumble when I do. Not to worry, I'll be back. Today you told me, "Shew!"

I'm a busy bee and honey is my thing.
When you hear me buzzing, my family's all I bring.

bee

You sit while waiting patiently, to share my honeycomb. You'll only get a sting or two and then go running home.

I'm a caring koala. I look like a bear to you. When you see me climbing, it's playtime at the zoo.

After nap I'm right back up, for eucalyptus leaves. I'm waiting for the rain to come, to catch my shower please.

koala

I'm a peeking peacock. I pick and peck and prance. When you see me strutting proud, my feathers spread to dance.

I like performing anxiously in front of a big crowd. But feeding me, is not a fee. In here that's not allowed.

peacock

I'm a tall giraffey. I stretch unto the sky.
I eat all things you can not reach, atop the mountain high.

giraffe

I neck around all day and night. My nose can't reach the ground. I'm much too big to fit a yard. So, I live far from town.

I'm a hefty elephant. I swing my nose upfront. When you see me stepping high, a ride is always fun.

elephant

I like to roam in open lands. Parade out to the sun. Just don't wait for my return, today is almost gone.

I'm a posing possum. I startle you at night. When you see me in your path, both you and I are fright.

possum

Ask yourself, "What do I do?" Run to the left, or right? It matters not. I'm on my way, to find my secret spot.

I'm an alligator. I'm looking for a friend. When you see me splashing, refuse to jump right in.

alligator

My smile is full of pearly teeth. My tail is strong and long. So, turn the music up and let's go dancing in the sun.

I'm a hopping bullfrog. I leap. I hop. I lounge. When you see me in the air, I'm headed to the ground.

bullfrog

At night I croak to find a mate. Until the morning comes. I may not be the smartest pet. But boy! I'm loads of fun.

I'm a slithering python. I look like a big worm. When you see me sliding, it's because I have no arms.

python

I manage well at climbing trees. I shed my skin to grow. I'm known for giving great big hugs, and that's how you show love.

I'm a licking lizard. I smell odd things on earth. When you see my tongue out, I probably sensed you first.

I like to hide when sun is out, it dries up my soft turf. I'm looking for the nearest pond, to quinch away my thirst.

lizard

I'm a raging rhino. As blind as I can be.
It's not my sight that you need fear. I smell just perfectly.

rhino

The horn that sits above my nose, will pierce the thickest skin. A head start's what you want from me. But only one to ten.

I'm a dashing deer, with my antlers all grown out. If you're camping in the woods, we'll both be on the scout.

When I catch a wind of you, I pause with much defense. You should take another route. I'm where the woods are dense.

deer

I'm a flippity fishy, I swim and play all day. When I'm home, I'm out to sea. At yours, I'm in a tank.

fish

Sometimes I stare out in the room and wish for your return. It's obvious, I need you when I want the TV on.

I'm a kicking kangaroo. I jump and box and pouch. When you interrupt me, I kick, and lights go out.

kangaroo

At your house, I can't jump high. The ceiling's in the way. The zoo is where you visit me, and there I'd like to stay.

I'm a pretty parakeet. I fly with much delight. At your house I'm in a cage, which makes it hard to fly.

You'd like to keep me as a pet How beautiful am I. My buddy, you may one day be. I might give you a try.

parakeet

I'm a purring kitty. I sneak. I pounce. I thrill. When you see me on the prowl, I'm trying to catch a meal.

I'd rather be all to myself, instead of constant hugs. Just leave my dish outside the door. I'm back before the morning.

kitten

I'm a fluffy puppy. I wag and bite and bark. When you see me in a stance, you hold out wide your arms.

I follow you from here to there and wait for your command. I'm your forever loving friend. More family than you planned.

puppy

Animals and insects are a big interest to humans, as we often are as curious of them, as we are ourselves. They can be cute and cutely, to fierce and aggressive. Nevertheless, from the beginning of time, we have searched for answers of where and how animals derived, to why and when some species went extinct.

Through endless efforts, scientists have studied the effect of human footprints or treatment of earth, by the animals that are becoming endangered and have gone extinct. Find your nearest zoo or aquarium to learn more, hands on experiences to the world of animals. Support a charity of your choice, to save a deserving, life.

?'s

Here are some answers to "What/Where?" questions, on the animals and insects in this book.

Lions live mainly in Africa.

Carnivore

The lion is the second in size of the felidae (cat) family. The males have a mane to make them appear larger. A full-grown male can be 6-7 feet long and as much as 2 feet at the shoulders while standing. Weighing 370-500 pounds. Females are the hunters of this family while also protecting the cubs from other predators and lions.

Diet include: rodents, baboons, buffalo, wildebeests, zebras and antelopes. Occasionally they can take down a baby giraffe or elephant.

The brown/grizzly bear lives in North America, Alaska and Canada.

The brown bear of North American was name grizzly. Large adult grizzlies can grow to 8 feet long and weigh up to 900 pounds. They have poor eyesight and put on a huge amounts of body fat in the winter. Brown bears hibernate (sleep) in what is called a den.

Omnivore

Diet includes berries, plant roots and shoots, small mammals, fish, carrion and the young calves of hoofed animals.

Spiders live all over the world. Except for Antartica and high elevation of the Himalayas.

The spider has over 46,700 species, with eight legs and has two body parts. They spin silk. Some species chase and overpower their prey, while others spin silk webs as a trap. Some use venom to quickly take their prey while others spin a silk-wrap around theirs. Spiders can be as small as 0.5mm to 90 mm and can be as long as 3.5 inches. Female spiders are generally larger than the males.

Carnivore

Diet includes other anthropoids: such as insects.

mostly Omnivores

other of the species
Herbivore and Carnivore

Some birds eat insects, others eat small mammals, some dive for fish. Others eat worms /invertebrates. Most eat seeds, fruits and nectar.

Birds live on every continent in the world.

Birds live everywhere on earth and have over 10,000 species. They are warm blooded vertebrates with feathers. Birds are considered to be related more so to reptiles than to mammals. The have wings and hatch eggs. Although they have great eyesight, their sense of smell is not as good. The wingspan of birds varies according to size. The smallest of the species is 2.5 inches long and can weigh less than 3 grams or 0.1 ounce. The largest of birds can be 9 feet tall and weigh up to 330 pounds. Not all birds have the ability to fly.

Ants live on every continent,
     except Antartica.

Omnivore

Ants are insects that grow to
.4 to 2 inches in length. There are
over 12,000 species and live all over
the world, especially hot climates.
They often have stings to defend
themselves. Ants live in social
complex colonies, which can have
more than one queen for breeding.
When ants bite in defense they
inject a chemical. Ants do not have
ears. They detect the vibrations
from the ground, through their feet
and can also lift more than 10-50
times their body weight. Ants
improve the quality of soil and
pollinate plants, which help the
ecosystem.

Diet incudes nectar,
seeds and insects.

Omnivore

Diet includes fruits, flowers, leaves, roots and fish.

Pigs live on every continent, except Antartica.

Pigs are mammals that originated from wild stock. They are called swine and also hog. The hoofs on the pig have even toes and they are able to squeal up to a decibel of 115. They have a great sense of smell, where in Europe are used to snout out truffles. They can range in size from 3-6 feet in length. The adult pig can weigh 110 to 770 pounds and as tall at 20.1 to 38.2 inches when standing. Pigs are bread to be consumed and have 3 types. One for lard weighing up to 220 pounds. The 2nd type is for bacon, weighing up to 150 pounds and the 3rd type of pig is for pork, weighing as much as 100 pounds.

Foxes live on every continent in the world.

Omnivore

Foxes are small mammals that belong to the dog family. There are twelve species of fox. They have a flat skull, pointed ears and a bushy tail. They also have great hearing. But foxes are considered to be pests because they attack humans and livestock on farms. A fox can be as tall as 14 to 20 inches and 18 to 35 inches in length. They live in the desert, grasslands and in the mountains and can weigh 15-31 pounds.

Diet includes insects, reptiles and birds.

Omnivore

Diet includes nectar and pollen from flowers.

Bees live on every continent, except Antartica.

Bees are insects. There are more than 20,000 kinds of bees. The adult bee range from 0.8 to 1.5 inches. Bees are most valuable because they pollinate. They also produce honey and wax products. Males do not share in the pollination or caring of the offspring. Duty lies with the female bees. Bees build their nests in the ground, woods, or in between twigs and canes. Bees can communicate the distance of food resources between each other. By doing a circular dance, it says food is within 250 feet. A wagging dance means food is farther from the hive.

Kaola's live in Australia.

Koalas are not bears. They live on the mainland and some islands. Koalas spend their lives living in a eucalyptus tree, where they sleep for more than 19 hours and only eat the leaves of the eucalyptus tree. The do not drink water, because they get it from the leaves of the tree. Koalas can weigh 20 pounds full grown and stand anywhere from 23.5 to 33.5 inches tall in size. Koalas have two thumbs on each hand, that are used to help them grip the trees. Their short stubby tails, pad them while sitting.

Herbivore

Diet includes eucalyptus leaves.

Omnivore

Diet include grains, seeds, small animals, fruits, flowers, berries and small reptiles, along with a variety of insects.

Peacocks live in India, Asia and Africa.

The peacock is in the bird family and is also called peafowl. There are three species of this pheasant family. The blue peafowl and the green peafowl live in India and Asia. The third kind of this species live in Africa and is called the Congo peafowl. The males are actually called a peacock. They have blue necks with bright colored green tail feathers, with spots that look lie eyes at the tip. The female is a peahen with a dull color of brown with green necks and cream colored heads. Peacocks can be very noisy and do lots of damage to property and crops. At night they use trees to avoid predators. They can be 36 to 90 inches in length weighing from 9 to 13 pounds.

Herbivore

Diet includes
shoots and leaves.

Giraffes live in East Africa, where the grasslands and open woodlands are.

Giraffes are the tallest living mammal on Earth and have only one species. Seven of its species have gone extinct. They have a very long neck with long legs. Their tongues can be 1 foot 7 inches long. The coat of the giraffe has two colors, brown divided by a lighter brown. Males weigh up to 4,260 lbs, while the female can weigh up to 2,600 lbs. Giraffe spend most of their lives standing up and only need five to thirty minutes of sleep, in a twenty-four-hour period. Every giraffe has a different pattern on their coats much like the fingerprints of humans. The tallest giraffe was measured to be 18 feet and 8 inches in 2019. Females grow to 14 feet. Giraffes use their long necks to wrestle and head butt when protecting their territories.

Elephants are native to Africa and South Asia.

Herbivore

It is the largest living land mammal. The elephant has two long, curved ivory tusks that are actually teeth. You can tell the species of elephant by their ears. There are three species of elephants. The African forest, the African savanna and the Asian elephant. A calf elephant can stand after 20 minutes and can walk within 1 hour. The elephants trunk weighs about 400 pounds, but can pick up a grain of rice with it. Elephants can live 60-70 years. At birth they can weigh 200 lbs and when full grown, up to 13,000 lbs, depending on the species.

Diet includes, tree bark, weeds, woody plants, grass and flowers

Oppssums live in the Americas and Possums live in Australia

The Opossum of the Americas are the same or similar as the possums that live in Australia. Possums have longer furry tails and Opossums have hairless tails. There are over 60 species of possums. Possums are scavengers that are considered to be a nuisance to humans. They grow up to 40 inches in length and have 50 teeth. Possums can weigh from less than an ounce to over 20 lbs and have a long tail, that is used for gripping leaves for making their bedding in nests. Many of the Opossums are immune to the venom of snakes, that they prey on. When scared a possum will play like it's dead.

Herbivore

Diet includes insects, rodents and plants

Omnivore

They live only in America, Mexico and China.

The alligator is a reptile. There are two species of alligator. The American and the Chinese alligator. They have powerful tails that are used to swim as well as for defense. Alligators can climb a tree or a fence with little trouble. An average American alligator can grow to 13 feet and weigh up to 790 lbs. But can also grow as much as 14 feet weighing up to 990 lbs. The Chinese alligator is considerably smaller at 7 feet in length, with the male only weighing about 100 lbs. Although the body is heavy, an alligator can move with speed, especially in short lunges. It pulls larger prey into the water and do a death roll, but they prefer smaller prey they can eat in one bite.

Diet includes other reptiles, fish and mammals.

The bullfrog lives in Canada and North America.

Omnivore

Bullfrogs are large frogs that are amphibian. The males have a loud croaking voice that is used when finding a mate. Bullfrogs live in swamps, ponds, and lakes. Don't be surprised to find a bullfrog in your pool, canals and in the ditches around your house. The body of the bullfrog is anywhere from 3.5 to 6 inches, the legs add 7 to 10 inches and they can weigh about 1.1 pounds. Depending on where they live, will determine their size. They eat anything they can put in their mouths.

Diet includes tadpoles, fish, small birds, and mice.

Pythons live in Asia, Africa and Australia.

Pythons are non-venomous reptiles. There are 42 species of pythons. They live in rainforest, grasslands, woodlands, swamps, dunes, shrubs and outcrops. A python's shelter is in tree branches, in abandoned burrows and under rocks. The smallest python species grow up to 24 inches and the larger of the species can grow up to 30 feet. The much needed camoflage of a python depends on the habitat they live in.

Carnivore

Diet includes for smaller: rodents, lizards and small birds. The bigger: mammals like monkeys, wallabies, antelope and pigs.

Lizards live across all continents, except Antartica and most oceanic islands.

Lizards are reptiles. There are over 6000 species of lizard. Lizards have a spiny rough skin, a short neck, four legs and a long tail. Some lizards live on ground, but they also live in trees as well as burrows. They are cold-blooded animals. Lizards weigh 10 to 30 grams. Some lizards do not grow more than several centimeters. The Komodo and Monitor lizard can average up to 10 feet and can prey on large animals, such as deer.

Carnivores, Herbivores and Omnivores
depends on type

Diet includes for carnivores only eat meat. Herbivores eat vegetables and fruit only, and omnivores meat and vegetables and fruit

Herbivore

Rhinos live in Africa and Asia

Diet includes grass, shrubs, leaves, fruits and trees.

Rhino's or rhinoceros are one of the largest mammals. There are 5 species of Rhino. Two live in Africa, the white and black rhino. Three live in Asia, the Sumatran, Javan and the great one-horned rhino. They all have a large horn in the front of its head, consisting of only keratin. Rhinos have either 1 or three toes on their feet or hoof. The black, Sumatran and the Javan species are endangered. The Largest is the White rhino. If they feel threatened, they will charge.

Herbivore

Diet includes grass, leaves and lichen.

Deer live in all continents, except Australia and Antartica.

Deer are hoofed mammals. There are 43 species of deer. Deers are found in dense forests, wetlands, mountains and plant areas. The male deer and only the female reindeer, grow new antlers every year. The exception is the Chinese water deer, which does not grow new antlers. They can grow to a height of 13 inches to 8.5 feet at the shoulders when standing. Depending on the species of deer, they range from 22 lbs to 440 lbs in size.

Most fish live in the ocean, lakes, rivers, and ponds. Some in fresh water, some in salt water.

Fish are cold-blooded vertebrae animals that live in water year-round and breath through their gills. There are more than 29,400 species of fish. They do not have limbs with digits, instead they have fins, along with scales all over their bodies to protect them. Fish can be as small as .3 inches to 39 feet 4 inches. Fish live in a variety of temperatures from 104 degrees Fahrenheit (hot) to 28 degrees Fahrenheit (cold).

Carnivores, Herbivores and Omnivores
depends on type

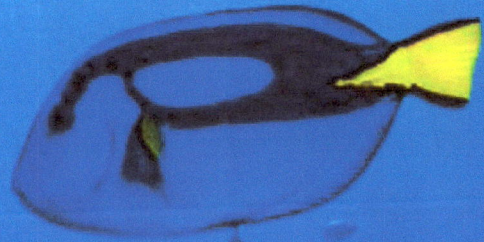

Diet includes leeches, small insects, worms, zooplankton, algae and smaller fish.

Kangaroo live in Australia and New Guinea

The Kangaroo is the largest of its marsupial family. It has large feet and very strong legs that are used to travel by leaping to get around. They also have a muscular long tail that is used for balance and a small head. The female kangaroos have a pouch where their offspring grow and nurse. There is an estimated 42.8 million kangaroos living in Australia. The males can grow to approximately 6 ft 7 inches and weigh up to 200 lbs. The females are smaller than the male kangaroo.

Herbivore

Diet includes grass, hypogeal fungi and shrubs.

Herbivore

Diet includes seed, fruit, vegetables and nuts

Parakeet are native to Australia.
Escaped pet parakeet live in Florida where the weather is warmer.

The parakeet is a small-medium sized parrot. They are curious birds that love to be entertained with toys and different games. Parakeet, have colorful feathers with long tails. They love to talk, sing and to mimic other sounds they hear. When they feel threatened, parakeet will bite. They can be messy and loud but love being social with people and their own kind. Parakeets grow to 6-7 inches in length with a wingspan of 10-12 inches. They can weigh about 30-40 grams by the time they are full grown.

Kittens live on every continent, except Antartica.

A kitten is a small cat. Although their eyesight is not very good, they do have a great sense of hearing and whiskers to feel and get around. Because they are born blind and are not able to regulate their own body temperatures, kittens are dependent on mom to help them. At birth, they weigh 3.5 oz and by two weeks 6-8 oz.

Omnivore

Diet includes milk from mom until 4 weeks then solids.

Omnivore

Diet includes mom's milk until 12 weeks

Puppies live on every continent, of the world.

A puppy is a young domesticated dog, that is less than one years old. There are 4 times as many puppies born to human babies each year. The fur of pups help regulate their body temperature and they are not born with teeth, By 4 weeks they start to grow teeth. A puppy's 28 baby teeth fall out by 16 weeks. When they are babies they spend most of their time sleeping and eating. Puppies range in size depending on the breed.

www.ingramcontent.com/pod-product-compliance
Lightning Source LLC
Chambersburg PA
CBHW060815270326
41930CB00002B/48